Yellow
Book
1

JUNIOR
READING Start

Iambooks

© 2011 I am Books

Published by

I am Books

327-32   1116ho, Daeroung Techno Town 12cha

Gasan-dong, Kumcheon-gu, Seoul, Korea 153-802

TEL 82-2-6343-0999

FAX 82-2-6343-0995~6

www.iambooks.co.kr

Publisher	Sangwook Oh, Sunghyun Shin
Author	TIMES CORE The Junior Times
Editor	Sungwon Lee, Dahhyun Gang, Jinhee Lee
Design	Mijung Oh, Ran Park
Illustrations	Soyoung Cho
Marketing	Shindong Jang, Shinkuk Jo, Jinhee Jung, Misun Jang

ISBN 978-89-6398-055-3 64740

Yellow
Book
1

JUNIOR
READING Start

How to Study This Book ??

01 Before reading articles, listen to audio files carefully two or three times.

02 Underline words that you are not familiar with, reading aloud the article.

03 Read the article one more time, making a guess the meaning of words.

04 Look up the dictionary to find out the meaning of words.

05 Memorize words that you don't know and try to solve the word tip quiz.

06 Read the article once again and answer the questions.

07 Lastly, listen to the audio file one more time focusing on the words you've learned.

CONTENTS

Which Is the Brightest Star?

Look up in the night sky. What can you see? Many stars are shining brightly! They are very beautiful. But do you know what the brightest star is? It is Sirius! The star is also called the "Dog Star." The star is made up of two bright stars – Sirius A and Sirius B.

Staff reporter Samuel Sohn

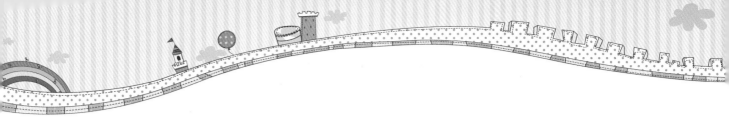

Writing

Let's look at the picture. Fill in the blanks and complete the sentences.

① star   ② shining   ③ up   ④ called   ⑤ see

(a) Look (   ) in the night sky.

(b) What can you (   )?

(c) Many stars are (   ) brightly.

(d) Which is the brightest (   )?

(e) It is Sirius (   ) the "Dog Star."

Word Tip

▮ look up	▮ shine	▮ 밝게	▮ 가장 밝은
_____	_____	_____	_____

▮ ~라고 불리다

_____

 **Grammar**

Circle the right word to complete each sentence.

(a) Have you ever [**see** / seen / seeing] stars at night?

(b) Stars shining brightly [**are** / is / have] very beautiful.

(c) Do you know [**when** / what / who] the brightest star is?

(d) The star is made up [**of** / from / in] two bright stars
— Sirius A and Sirius B.

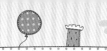

 **Vocabulary**

Find the words used in the story in the puzzle below.

M	A	G	L	Z	X	W	D	R	O
G	D	O	Q	D	C	Y	A	V	I
N	J	G	T	Y	G	C	K	C	E
G	I	G	F	E	F	U	P	S	M
C	T	G	N	G	U	E	I	T	A
V	V	Y	H	E	F	R	F	A	N
O	I	C	K	T	H	G	I	R	B
I	U	A	C	R	L	W	Q	H	E
P	R	A	U	I	P	Y	T	G	F
Q	X	S	I	R	I	U	S	L	D

Words

NIGHT / SKY / STAR

BRIGHT / SIRIUS

Hula - Hooping Helps You Stay in Shape

Hula-hooping is a lot of fun. It is also good for your health! It is a simple, easy, and fun way to stay active. Try to hula-hoop with your family. It will be more fun! It is also a great way to spend time with your family. You can also invite your friends over and hula-hoop together. When you do it, don't forget to play fun music!

Staff reporter Erica Choi

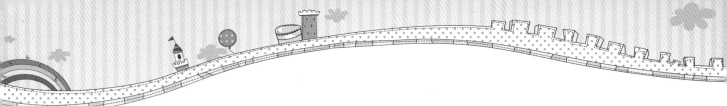

Complete the sentences by filling in the blanks.

(a) Hula-**h** __ __ __ __ __ __ is a lot of fun and it's **g** __ __ __ for your health!

(b) Try to hula-hoop with your **f** __ __ __ __ __.

(c) It is a **g** __ __ __ __ way to **s** __ __ __ __ time with your family.

(d) You can also **i** __ __ __ __ __ your friends **o** __ __ __ and hula-hoop together.

Word Tip

▌ hula-hoop	▌ a lot of fun	▌ be good for	▌ simple
_____	_____	_____	_____
▌ easy	▌ stay active	▌ ~하도록 노력하다	▌ ~와 시간을 보내다
_____	_____	_____	_____
▌ ~을 초대하다	▌ 함께	▌ ~하는 것을 잊다	
_____	_____	_____	

Vocabulary I

Let's complete the crossword puzzle.

Words

YOUR (▶) / SPEND (▶) / INVITE (▼) / WITH (▶)
HULA-HOOP (▼) / FUN (▶) / ACTIVE (▶)

Vocabulary Ⅱ

Let's find the matching words.

| active | spend | invite | family | music |

(a) 시간을 보내다   (   )

(b) 음악   (   )

(c) 활발한   (   )

(d) 가족   (   )

(e) 초대하다   (   )

Comprehension

Circle O if the statement is true, and circle X if it is false.

(a) Hula-hooping is a lot of fun.   O / X

(b) You can try hula-hooping with your family.   O / X

(c) You can hula-hoop with your friends.   O / X

(d) Don't play music when hula-hooping. You may fall down.   O / X

Drink Milk for Your Bones

Do you drink milk every day? Doctors say that children need to drink two glasses of milk a day. Milk is good for your bones. It is rich in calcium. It makes your bones strong. Milk also helps your growth. Start drinking milk today. Then, your bones will say "Thank you!"

Staff reporter Erica Choi

Vocabulary I

Read each question and find the right answer.

(a) What is the main topic of the article?

① France

② Milk

③ Chocolate

④ Rabbits

(b) Write down three words that begin with "M"!

① _____

② _____

③ _____

(c) Who is a person that works at the hospital?

D __ c t __ __

Word Tip

▮ a glass of	▮ be good for	▮ bone	▮ be rich in
_____	_____	_____	_____

▮ 칼슘	▮ 튼튼한	▮ 성장
_____	_____	_____

 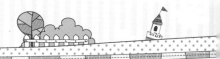

 **Vocabulary Ⅱ**

Choose the right word to complete each sentence.

(a) Children need to drink two glasses of _____.

① cheese   ② cola

③ milk   ④ water

(b) Milk is good for your _____.

① cat   ② bones

③ dogs   ④ video games

(c) Milk also helps your _____.

① hair   ② clothes

③ eye   ④ growth

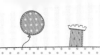
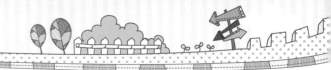

 **Comprehension**

Look at the picture below and then answer the questions about it.

(a) What is the girl drinking?

① Coffee

② Water

③ Coke

④ Milk

(b) What color is her hair?

① Blonde

② Brown

③ White

④ Green

(c) What part of the body is milk good for?

① Bones

② Fingers

③ Back

④ Hair

The Largest Chocolate Bar in the World

On September 11, the world's largest chocolate bar was born in Armenia. Measuring 5.6 meters by 2.75 meters, the chocolate bar weighs 4,410 kilograms! It is 25 centimeters thick. It is so huge! Don't you want to taste the world's largest chocolate bar? I do!

Staff reporter Samuel Sohn

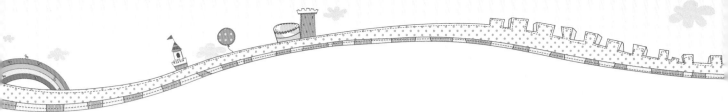

 **Question** **Comprehension**

Which is NOT true about the article?

(a) The world's smallest chocolate bar was born in Armenia.

(b) The chocolate bar weighs 4,410 kilograms.

(c) The chocolate bar is 25 centimeters thick.

(d) The chocolate bar is so huge.

Word Tip			
▍the largest	▍be born	▍Armenia	▍거대한, 큰
▍무게가 ~이다	▍두께가 ~인, 두꺼운	▍측정하다, (길이, 양, 치수 등이) ~이다	
▍맛보다			

 **Question** **Grammar**

Circle the right words to complete each sentence.

(a) The world's largest chocolate bar was opened in public [**in** / **on** / **at**] September 11.

(b) Dark chocolate can be good [**at** / **for** / **from**] your body.

(c) There are [**much** / **most** / **many**] kinds of chocolates in the world.

(d) [**Don't** / **Wasn't** / **Will**] you want to taste the world's largest chocolate bar?

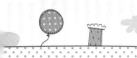

Writing

Look at the picture below. Complete the sentences to answer the questions.

(a) What is it? → It is a _____.

(b) Where was it born? → It was born in _____.

(c) Why was it special? → Because it was the _____
chocolate bar.

Vocabulary

Let's think of some words or phrases that could be used to describe chocolate. Fill in the blanks.

(a) It is **s** __ __ __ __.

(b) It is usually black in **c** __ __ __ __.

(c) It is **l** __ __ __ __ __ by children.

(d) When you are stressed, it can help you to feel **b** __ __ __ __ __.

Health: Do Not Touch Your Pet's Food Dish!

Many families keep pets at home. If you keep a pet at home, don't feed it in the kitchen. Its food dish can make you sick! American doctors found that pet food may carry salmonella. Salmonella is a disease caused by bacteria in food. Salmonella causes food poisoning. Keep your pet's food dish clean and away from the kitchen!

Staff reporter Erica Choi

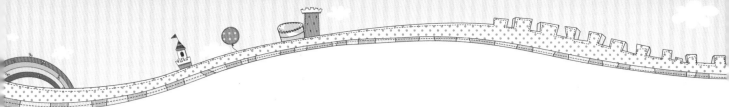

01 Question **Writing**

Complete the sentences by filling in the blanks.

(a) Many families **k** __ __ __ **p** __ __ __ at home.

(b) Its food dish can make you **s** __ __ __ !

(c) Salmonella is a **d** __ __ __ __ __ __ caused by bacteria in food.

(d) Keep your pet's food dish clean and away from the **k** __ __ __ __ __ __ !

Word Tip

▌pet	▌feed	▌dish	▌아픈
_____	_____	_____	_____
▌(병을) 옮기다, 운반하다	▌disease	▌일으키다	▌food poisoning
_____	_____	_____	_____
▌박테리아	▌부엌	▌깨끗한	
_____	_____	_____	

 ## Vocabulary I

Let's complete the crossword puzzle.

Words

CARRY (▼) / CLEAN (▶) / CAUSE (▼)

KITCHEN (▼) / BACTERIA (▶)

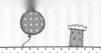
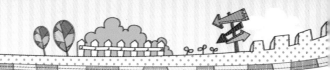

 **Question** **Vocabulary Ⅱ**

Let's find the matching words.

feed   kitchen   carry   food poisoning   cause

(a) 주방   (   )

(b) 식중독   (   )

(c) 먹이를 주다   (   )

(d) 일으키다   (   )

(e) 운반하다   (   )

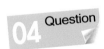 **Question** **Comprehension**

Circle O if the statement is true, and circle X if the statement is false.

(a) If you keep a pet at home, it is okay to feed it in the kitchen.   O / X

(b) Pet food may carry salmonella that causes food poisoning.   O / X

(c) Many families keep pets at home.   O / X

(d) Keep your pet's food dish clean and away from your room.   O / X

Which Is the Largest Bird in the World?

There are many kinds of birds in the world. Do you know which bird is the world's largest? It's the ostrich! It lives in Africa. This bird cannot fly! But it has long, strong legs. It can run very fast. This bird eats plants and seeds. But it can also eat insects and even lizards!

Staff reporter Samuel Sohn

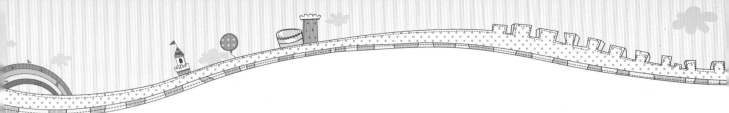

Comprehension

Look at the sentences below and decide whether they are true (o) or false (x).

(a) The ostrich is the largest bird in the world.　　　　　　　O / X

(b) The ostrich lives in America.　　　　　　　　　　　　　O / X

(c) The ostrich can fly as fast as the airplane.　　　　　　　O / X

(d) The ostrich eats plants, seeds, and even lizards.　　　　　O / X

Word Tip

▮ kind	▮ the largest	▮ ostrich	▮ live in
―――――	―――――	―――――	―――――
▮ fly	▮ strong	▮ 다리	▮ 식물
―――――	―――――	―――――	―――――
▮ 씨앗	▮ 곤충	▮ 심지어	▮ 도마뱀
―――――	―――――	―――――	―――――

 **Grammar**

Circle the right words to complete each sentence.

(a) There are many kinds [**of** / to / for] birds in the world.

(b) This bird cannot fly but [**we** / it / they] has long, strong legs.

(c) The ostrich lives [**at** / on / in] Africa.

(d) Do you know which bird [**was** / is / are] the world's largest?

03 Question **Writing**

Look at the picture below. Complete the sentences to answer the questions.

(a) What is this? → It is a _____.

(b) Where is a baby ostrich? → The baby ostrich is inside _____.

(c) What does it eat? → It eats _____.

04 Question **Vocabulary**

Let's think of some words or phrases that could be used to describe ostrich. Fill in the blanks.

(a) It is a very **la** __ __ __ bird.

(b) It cannot **f** __ __.

(c) It has **st** __ __ __ __ legs.

(d) It can **r** __ __ very fast.

Eat Less Butter for Your Heart!

Many children enjoy eating butter. Some children eat bread and butter for breakfast. Well, butter makes your bread taste very good. But doctors say that eating butter is not good for your heart. Butter is high in bad fat. If you eat too much butter, it can cause heart disease. Margarine is a better choice than butter.

Staff reporter Daniel Chang

Comprehension

Let's look at the picture and fill in the blanks.

Hint: Answers are in the article.

(a) It is a piece of _____.

(b) Some _____ are spread on the _____.

(c) Butter makes our bread _____ good.

(d) But according to doctors, eating butter is not good for our _____.

(e) Butter is _____ in bad fat.

Word Tip

▮ enjoy	▮ butter	▮ breakfast	▮ taste
_____	_____	_____	_____
▮ heart	▮ be high in	▮ 지방	▮ 유발하다
_____	_____	_____	_____
▮ 심장병	▮ 마가린	▮ 선택	
_____	_____	_____	

Vocabulary

Connect each picture to the correct meaning.

breakfast

ⓐ

① The thing contained in food such as meat, oil and cheese

fat

ⓑ

② The first meal of the day

disease

ⓒ

③ A kind of illness

 **Writing**

Look at the picture below and write your own answers.

Hint: Be creative!

(a) What is he doing?

→ He is _____.

(b) Do you think it is good to eat too much butter for your health?

→ I think it's _____ good to eat too much butter.

(c) Which one can be better choice than butter?

→ _____

_____.

How Many States Are There in America?

America is a very big country. It is 42 times bigger than Korea. The country has many states. There are 50 states in America. Delaware is the country's first state. Then, where is America's last state? It's Hawaii! The beautiful island became America's 50th state in 1959.

Staff reporter Daniel Chang

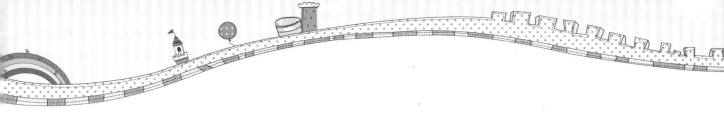

Fill in the blanks with the right words.

country / 1959 / states / bigger
island / Korea / many / last

(a) America is a big _____.

(b) There are 50 _____ in America.

(c) Hawaii is a beautiful _____.

Word Tip

▌country	▌time	▌bigger	▌than
_____	_____	_____	_____
▌state	▌Delaware	▌첫째의	▌그러면
_____	_____	_____	_____
▌마지막의	▌섬	▌~이 되다	
_____	_____	_____	

 **Comprehension**

Look at the sentences below and decide whether they are true (O) or false (X).

(a) Korea is 42 times bigger than America.   O / X

(b) Delaware is America's first state.   O / X

(c) Hawaii became an American state in 1959.   O / X

 **Vocabulary** Ⅰ

Choose the right word to complete each sentence.

(a) Korea is a beautiful [**country** / state / hot dog].

(b) Hawaii is a [**bicycle** / country / state].

(c) Islands are surrounded by [**trees** / water / songs].

 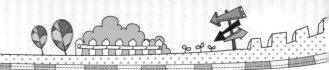

Vocabulary II

Let's find the words from the story in this word puzzle!

D	P	D	P	Q	Z	H	E	G	I
E	V	N	A	N	S	Q	A	I	L
N	V	A	A	C	A	N	A	W	B
Q	R	L	R	Y	I	W	I	V	O
G	O	S	U	A	A	R	G	Z	Q
O	R	I	P	H	G	H	E	A	H
H	D	Y	H	C	T	D	A	M	M
S	T	A	T	E	Z	O	T	S	A
Z	R	J	H	D	Q	H	I	S	B
Y	R	T	N	U	O	C	F	C	D

Words

ISLAND / STATE / COUNTRY / HAWAII / AMERICA

Which Country Will Hold the Next World Cup?

The 2010 World Cup is over. It was held in South Africa. Many soccer fans visited the country to watch the games. The World Cup is held every 4 years. The next World Cup will be held in 2014. So, which country will hold the event? Brazil! Let's visit Brazil to cheer for our players!

Staff reporter Erica Choi

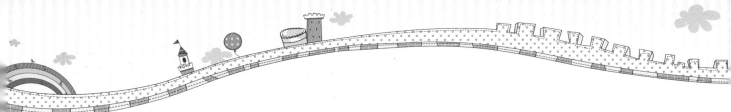

Vocabulary I

Read each question and find the right answer.

(a) What is the main topic of the article?

① The next World Cup

② The origin of the World Cup

③ The winner of the World Cup

④ The advantage of the World Cup

(b) Write down three words that begin with "C" in the article.

① _____

② _____

③ _____

(c) Which country will hold the next World Cup?

B __ __ __ __ __

Word Tip

finally	over	be held	soccer fan
_____	_____	_____	_____
visit	매 4년 마다	열다, 개최하다	행사
_____	_____	_____	_____
~를 응원하다	선수		
_____	_____		

 # Vocabulary II

Choose the right word to complete each sentence.

(a) The 2010 World Cup is finally over. It was _____ in South Africa.

① host

② held

③ called

④ chosen

(b) Many soccer fans _____ the country to watch the games.

① visited

② invited

③ lived

④ saw

(c) Let's visit Brazil to _____ for our players!

① select

② choose

③ play

④ cheer

40

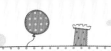

03 Question ▾ **Comprehension**

Look at the picture below and then answer the questions about it.

(a) What is the man holding with his fingers?

   ① paper   ② newspaper

   ③ bread   ④ book

(b) What is written on the paper the man is holding?

   ① Spain   ② Korea

   ③ Brazil   ④ Japan

(c) What kind of hairstyle does the man have?

   ① straight   ② curly

   ③ pony tail   ④ bald

UNIT 10

Doorknobs Are Full of Germs!

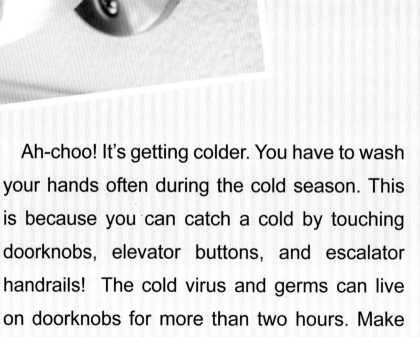

Ah-choo! It's getting colder. You have to wash your hands often during the cold season. This is because you can catch a cold by touching doorknobs, elevator buttons, and escalator handrails! The cold virus and germs can live on doorknobs for more than two hours. Make sure to wash your hands with soap after touching them.

Staff reporter Daniel Chang

42

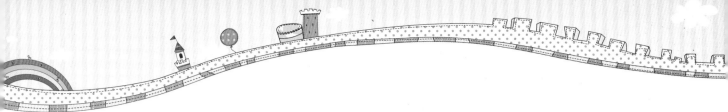

Fill in the blanks with the right words.

listen / catch / soap / clean
wash / sure

(a) You have to _____ your hands often during the cold season.

(b) You can _____ a cold by touching doorknobs, elevator buttons, and escalator handrails!

(c) Make _____ to wash your hands with soap after touching doorknobs.

Word Tip

ǁ ah-choo	ǁ get colder	ǁ have to	ǁ wash one's hands
ǁ season	ǁ catch a cold	ǁ touch	ǁ 손잡이
ǁ 엘리베이터 버튼	ǁ 에스컬레이터 난간	ǁ 감기 바이러스	ǁ 세균

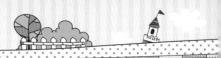

 **Comprehension**

Look at the sentences below and decide whether they are true (O) or false (X).

(a) The weather gets warmer in the winter.   O / X

(b) Make sure to wash your hands with soap after touching   O / X
   doorknobs.

(c) The cold virus and germs can live on doorknobs for more   O / X
   than two hours.

 **Grammar**

Choose the right word to complete each sentence.

(a) The cold virus and germs can live on doorknobs for more [as / than / of]
   two hours.

(b) Make sure to wash your hands [with / in / on] soap after touching
   them.

(c) You can catch a cold [as / by / if] touching doorknobs, elevator buttons,
   and escalator handrails.

04 Question Vocabulary

Let's find the words from the story in this word puzzle!

H	T	U	I	L	O	P	B	V	N
G	E	R	M	H	T	W	E	G	J
M	N	H	Q	A	C	A	R	D	E
C	V	B	N	M	O	E	Y	H	G
A	E	F	G	T	L	B	V	V	K
C	X	H	A	N	D	R	A	I	L
Y	U	J	K	L	G	F	D	R	W
G	Y	U	I	F	J	N	C	U	W
F	U	Y	N	O	S	A	E	S	R
A	S	F	G	H	N	J	K	O	T

Words

COLD / SEASON / HANDRAIL / VIRUS / GERM

Are There Birds That Cannot Fly?

What is your favorite bird? There are many kinds of birds in the world. Birds have wings and they can fly. But did you know that some birds cannot fly? Ostriches and penguins are birds.But they cannot fly! Kiwi birds that live in New Zealand cannot fly, either. Why don't you learn more about these interesting birds with your friends?

Staff reporter Samuel Sohn

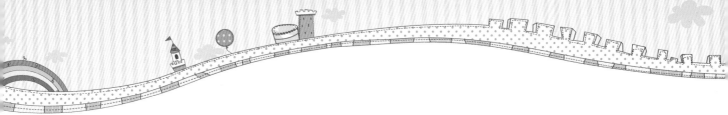

Comprehension

Look at the sentences below and decide whether they are true (o) or false (x).

(a) Birds have wings.   O / X

(b) Ostriches are not birds.   O / X

(c) Kiwi birds live in New Zealand.   O / X

(d) Kiwi birds can fly.   O / X

Word Tip

▌favorite	▌kind	▌wing	▌fly
_____	_____	_____	_____
▌ostrich	▌penguin	▌키위	▌또한, 역시 (부정문에서)
_____	_____	_____	_____
▌~하는 것이 어때?	▌배우다		
_____	_____		

 **Grammar**

Circle the right words to complete each sentence.

(a) What is [**your** / you / yours] favorite bird?

(b) There are many kinds of birds [**at** / in / from] the world.

(c) Penguins are birds but [it / **they** / we] cannot fly.

(d) Why don't you learn [most / less / **more**] about these interesting birds with your friend?

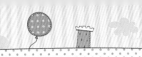 

Writing

Look at the picture below. Complete the sentences to answer the questions.

(a) What is it? → It is a _____.

(b) Where does it live? → It lives in _____.

(c) What birds cannot fly? → _____
cannot fly.

Vocabulary

Let's think of some words or phrases that could be used to describe Penguin. Fill in the blanks.

(a) It is a **b** __ __ __.

(b) It cannot **f** __ __.

(c) It usually **l** __ __ __ __ in the Antarctic.

(d) It is good at **s** __ __ __ __ __ __ __.

Turn the Volume Down!

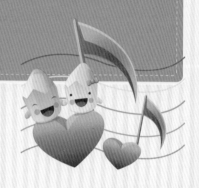

Music makes you happy. But you have to be careful when using earphones or headphones. If you listen to music too loud, it can hurt your ears and cause hearing problems. Don't listen to music through earphones for more than an hour a day. When listening to music, turn the volume down to protect your ears.

Staff reporter Daniel Chang

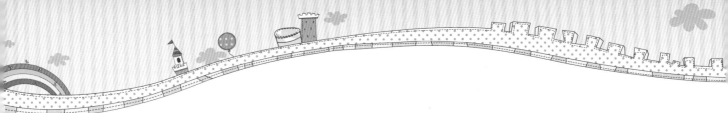

01 Question ▷ Writing

Fill in the blanks with the right words.

remain / loud / sound / hear
volume / careful

(a) You should be _____ when using earphones or headphones.

(b) Listening to music too _____ can hurt your ears.

(c) Turn the _____ down to protect your ears.

Word Tip

‖ have to	‖ be careful	‖ earphone	‖ headphone
_____	_____	_____	_____
‖ loud	‖ 아프게(다치게)하다	‖ ~을 유발하다, ~의 원인이 되다	‖ 청력 장애, 청각 문제
_____	_____	_____	_____
‖ 하루에 한 시간 이상	‖ 볼륨(음량)을 낮추다	‖ 보호하다	
_____	_____	_____	

 Comprehension

Look at the sentences below and decide whether they are true (o) or false (x).

(a) Listening to music loud will make your ears more healthy.　　O / X

(b) Don't listen to music through earphones for more than an hour a day.　　O / X

(c) Earphones and headphones make listening to music safe.　　O / X

 Vocabulary I

Choose the right word to complete each sentence.

(a) If you listen to music too loud, it can hurt your [**eyes** / **nose** / ears].

(b) When listening to music, turn the volume [**circle** / **down** / up].

(c) If you hurt your ears, it can [**cause** / **reason** / take] hearing problems.

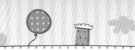

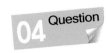

Vocabulary II

Let's find the words from the story in this word puzzle!

A	X	C	V	R	T	J	U	I	A
H	B	D	F	G	H	G	R	T	S
Y	V	H	A	P	P	Y	A	H	D
U	H	F	G	V	B	N	M	O	Y
I	G	H	L	W	E	R	K	U	U
P	T	U	O	U	I	O	B	R	M
M	R	M	U	S	I	C	B	N	H
K	P	I	D	O	W	N	R	H	Y
L	L	J	H	G	R	T	U	I	O
U	I	K	D	F	E	G	H	J	N

Words

HAPPY / MUSIC / LOUD / HOUR / DOWN

Which Is the Biggest Island in the World?

There are many islands in the world. But do you know what the world's biggest island is? It's Greenland! The island belongs to Denmark. The capital of Greenland is Nuuk. Most of the people who live on the island are Eskimos. Unlike its name, Greenland is covered with ice and snow. What an interesting island!

Staff reporter Daniel Chang

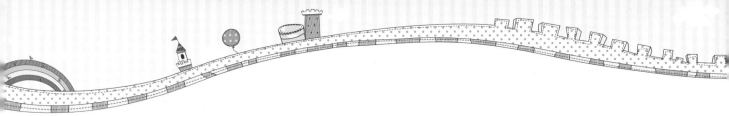

Use the words below when you make the sentences.

island

igloo

Eskimo

ice

snow

cover

jump

Greenland

(a) What is this?

→ This is _____.

(b) Where can we find this?

→ We can find _____.

(c) Why is the top of the igloo smashed?

→ A penguin _____.

Word Tip			
▮ island	▮ the biggest	▮ Greenland	▮ belong to
_____	_____	_____	_____
▮ 수도	▮ 에스키모인	▮ ~와는 달리	▮ ~로 덮여 있다
_____	_____	_____	_____

02 Question Vocabulary I

Circle the right words to make the sentence correct.

(a) The island belongs [**on** / **to** / into] Denmark.

(b) The [**capital** / flag / song] of Greenland is Nuuk.

(c) [**Unlike** / Like / Likely] its name, Greenland is covered with ice and snow.

(d) [**Most** / Least / Less] of the people who live on the island are Eskimos.

03 Question Writing II

Write your own story describing the picture below.

Hint: Be creative!

Why is this penguin jumping from a cliff?

_____

_____

_____

_____

_____

_____

_____

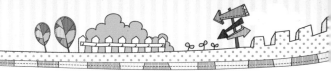

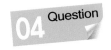 **Vocabulary II**

Let's finish the cross word puzzle below related to the story.

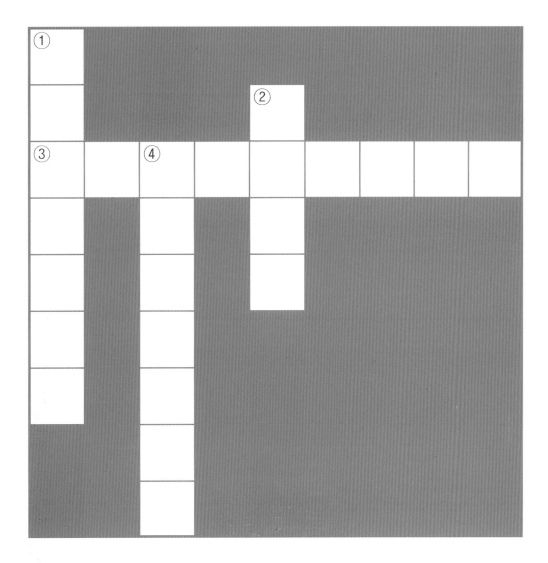

Across

③ The biggest island in the world

Down

① The opposite of smallest

② It comes down from the sky when it is very cold

④ People who live on the world's biggest island

What Is the Biggest Country in Europe?

There are many countries in Europe – 44 countries in total. So, what is the biggest country in Europe? Let me give you some hints: the country's language is French, its capital is Paris and the city is famous for the Eiffel Tower. Yes, it's France! You may think that Russia is the biggest country in Europe but Russia belongs to Eurasia.

Staff reporter Samuel Sohn

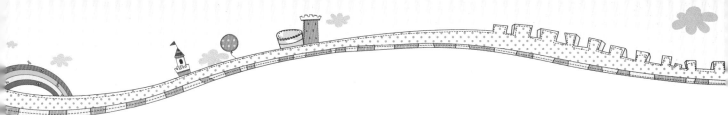

Comprehension

Which is NOT true about Europe?
Read the following sentences and then correct the wrong one.

(a) There are 40 countries in Europe.   **O / X**

→ _____

(b) The biggest country in Europe is Russia.   **O / X**

→ _____

(c) France's capital is Paris.   **O / X**

→ _____

(d) Russia belongs to Eurasia.   **O / X**

→ _____

Word Tip

▌country	▌Europe	▌in total	▌the biggest
_____	_____	_____	_____
▌give a hint	▌언어	▌프랑스어	▌수도
_____	_____	_____	_____
▌~로 유명하다	▌에펠탑		
_____	_____		

 **Grammar**

Circle the right words to complete each sentence.

(a) What is the [**biggest** / **bigger** / **big**] country in Europe?

(b) Paris is famous [**of** / **for** / **at**] the Eiffel Tower.

(c) Have you ever [**visit** / **visiting** / **visited**] France?

(d) The country's language [**is** / **are** / **was**] French.

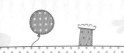 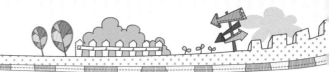

Writing

Look at the picture below. Complete the sentences to answer the questions.

(a) What is it? → It is the _____.

(b) Where was it built? → It was built in _____.

(c) Why is it special? → Because it is the _____
in Paris, France.

Vocabulary

Let's think of some words or phrases that could be used to describe France. Fill in the blanks.

(a) It belongs to **E** __ __ __ __ __.

(b) It is the most **b** __ __ __ __ __ __ country in Europe.

(c) The Eiffel Tower in Paris is 300 meters **t** __ __ __.

(d) 30 countries in the world use the **F** __ __ __ __ __ language.

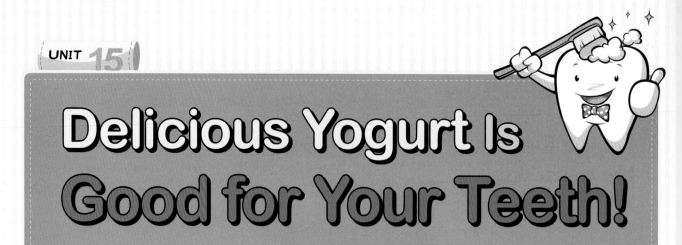

Delicious Yogurt Is Good for Your Teeth!

A new study from Japan said that eating yogurt makes children's teeth healthy. Try to eat yogurt 4 times a week. It will protect your teeth from decay. There are many kinds of delicious yogurt you can choose from. Enjoy yogurt for your teeth!

Staff reporter Daniel Chang

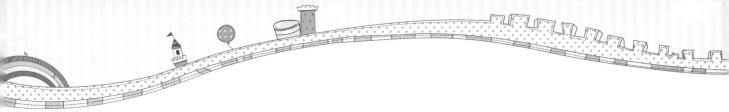

Vocabulary I

Let's look at the picture and fill in the blanks.

Hint: Answers are in the article.

(a) The _____ looks delicious.

(b) According to the new study, yogurt is good for your _____.

(c) It can keep your teeth from _____.

(d) It's good to eat yogurt four _____ a week.

Word Tip

study	yogurt	healthy	try to
_____	_____	_____	_____
time	protect	충치	종류
_____	_____	_____	_____
맛있는	선택하다	즐기다	
_____	_____	_____	

 ## Vocabulary II

Connect each picture to the correct meaning.

healthy

ⓐ

① Having or showing good health

protect

ⓑ

② If this happens to your teeth, your teeth are gradually destroyed

decay

ⓒ

③ To guard someone from being harmed or damaged

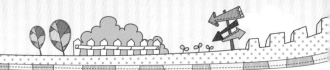

 **Writing**

Look at the picture below and write your own answers.

Hint: Be creative!

(a) What is she doing?

→ She is _____.

(b) What do you think is the flavor of the yogurt that she is eating?

→ It looks like _____ yogurt.

(c) Do you enjoy eating yogurt? If so, what kind of flavor do you like the most?

→ Yes, I enjoy _____

_____.

ANSWERS

Word Tip

(올려다) 보다 / 빛나다 / brightly / the brightest / be called

1. Writing
(a) ③
(b) ⑤
(c) ②
(d) ①
(e) ④

2. Grammar
(a) seen
(b) are
(c) what
(d) of

3. Vocabulary

```
M A G L Z X W D R O
G D O Q D C Y A V I
N J G T Y G C K C E
G I F E F U P S M
C T G N G U E I T A
V V Y H E F R F A N
O I C K T H G I R B
I U A C R L W Q H E
P R A U I P Y T G F
Q X S I R I U S L D
```

---

2. Vocabulary I

```
H
F U N   W I T H
L       N
A C T I V E
H       I
Y O U R   T
O         E
S P E N D
```

3. Vocabulary II
(a) spend
(b) music
(c) active
(d) family
(e) invite

4. Comprehension
(a) O
(b) O
(c) O
(d) X

Word Tip

한 잔 / ~에 좋다 / 뼈 / ~이 풍부하다 / calcium / strong / growth

1. Vocabulary I
(a) ②
(b) Mouse / Magic / Mouth
(c) Doctor

2. Vocabulary II
(a) ③
(b) ②
(c) ④

3. Comprehension
(a) ④
(b) ②
(c) ①

Word Tip

가장 큰 / 태어나다 / 아르메니아 / huge / weigh / thick / measure / taste

1. Comprehension
(a)

2. Grammar
(a) on
(b) for
(c) many
(d) Don't

3. Writing
(a) chocolate bar
(b) Armenia
(c) world's largest

4. Vocabulary
(a) sweet
(b) color
(c) loved
(d) better

Word Tip

애완동물 / 먹이다 / 음식 / sick / carry / (질)병 / cause / 식중독 / bacteria / kitchen / clean

1. Writing
(a) keep, pets
(b) sick
(c) disease
(d) kitchen

Word Tip

훌라후프를 돌리다 / 정말 재미있는 (것) / ~에 좋다 / 간단한 / 쉬운 / 활동적으로 지내다 / try to / spend time with / invite / together / forget (to)

1. Writing
(a) hooping, good
(b) family
(c) great, spend
(d) invite, over

2. Vocabulary I

3. Vocabulary II
(a) kitchen
(b) food poisoning
(c) feed
(d) cause
(e) carry

4. Comprehension
(a) X
(b) O
(c) O
(d) X

 UNIT 16

Word Tip

종류 / 가장 큰 / 타조 / ~에 살다 /
날다 / 강한, 힘이 센 / leg / plant /
seed / insect / even / lizard

1. Comprehension
(a) O
(b) X
(c) X
(d) O

2. Grammar
(a) of
(b) it
(c) in
(d) is

3. Writing
(a) baby ostrich

(b) an egg
(c) plants, seeds, insects and
even lizards

4. Vocabulary
(a) large
(b) fly
(c) strong
(d) run

 UNIT 17

Word Tip

즐기다 / 버터 / 아침식사 / 맛이 나다 /
심장 / ~이 높다 / fat / cause /
heart disease / margarine / choice

1. Comprehension
(a) bread
(b) butter, bread
(c) taste
(d) heart
(e) high

2. Vocabulary
ⓐ – ②
ⓑ – ①
ⓒ – ③

3. Writing
(a) eating some bread
(b) not
(c) Margarine can be better
choice than butter.

 UNIT 18

Word Tip

나라, 국가 / (몇) 배 / 더 큰 / ~보다 /
주 / 델라웨어(주) / first / then / last /
island / become

1. Writing
(a) country
(b) states
(c) island

2. Comprehension
(a) X
(b) O
(c) O

3. Vocabulary I
(a) country
(b) state
(c) water

4. Vocabulary II

 UNIT 19

Word Tip

마침내 / 끝난 / 열리다 / 축구팬 /
방문하다 / every 4 years / hold /
event / cheer for / player

1. Vocabulary I
(a) ①
(b) cup / country / cheer
(c) Brazil

2. Vocabulary II
(a) ②
(b) ①
(c) ④

3. Comprehension
(a) ①
(b) ③
(c) ④

UNIT 10

Word Tip

에취 / 더 추워지다 / ~해야만 한다 /
손을 씻다 / 계절 / 감기에 걸리다 /
만지다 / doorknob / elevator button /
escalator handrail / cold virus /
germ

1. Writing
(a) wash
(b) catch
(c) sure

2. Comprehension
(a) X
(b) O
(c) O

3. Grammar
(a) than
(b) with
(c) by

4. Vocabulary

H	T	U	I	L	O	P	B	V	N
G	E	R	M	H	T	W	E	G	J
M	N	H	Q	A	C	A	R	D	E
C	V	B	N	M	O	E	Y	H	G
A	E	F	G	T	L	B	V	V	K
C	X	H	A	N	D	R	A	I	L
Y	U	J	K	L	G	F	D	R	W
G	Y	U	I	F	J	N	C	U	W
F	U	Y	N	O	S	A	E	S	R
A	S	F	G	H	N	J	K	O	T

UNIT 11

Word Tip

매우 좋아하는 / 종류 / 날개 / 날다 /
타조 / 펭귄 / Kiwi / either /
Why don't you ~ ? / learn

1. Comprehension
(a) O
(b) X
(c) O
(d) X

2. Grammar
(a) your
(b) in
(c) they
(d) more

3. Writing
(a) kiwi bird
(b) New Zealand
(c) Ostriches and penguins
     and kiwi birds

4. Vocabulary
(a) bird
(b) fly
(c) lives
(d) swimming

UNIT 12

Word Tip

~해야만 한다 / 조심하다 / 이어폰 /
헤드폰 / 큰, 시끄러운 / hurt / cause /
hearing problem /
more than an hour a day /
turn the volume down / protect

1. Writing
(a) careful
(b) loud
(c) volume

2. Comprehension
(a) X
(b) O
(c) X

3. Vocabulary I
(a) ears
(b) down
(c) cause

4. Vocabulary II

A	X	C	V	R	T	J	U	I	A
H	B	D	F	G	H	G	R	T	S
Y	V	H	A	P	P	Y	A	H	D
U	H	F	G	V	B	N	M	O	Y
I	G	H	L	W	E	R	K	U	U
P	T	U	O	U	I	O	B	R	M
M	R	M	U	S	I	C	B	N	H
K	P	I	D	O	W	N	R	H	Y
L	L	J	H	G	R	T	U	I	O
U	I	K	D	F	E	G	H	J	N

UNIT 13

Word Tip

섬 / 가장 큰 / 그린란드 / ~에 속하다 /
capital / Eskimo / unlike /
be covered with

1. Writing I
(a) an igloo.
(b) this in Greenland.
(c) jumped up and down on it.

2. Vocabulary I
(a) to
(b) capital
(c) Unlike
(d) Most

3. Writing II
The penguin is preparing for a diving competition. The competition is held every year. If he wins the first prize, he will receive lots of fish. He is jumping from the cliff to practice his diving.

4. Vocabulary II

Word Tip

나라, 국가 / 유럽 / 통틀어 / 가장 큰 /
힌트를 주다 / language / French /
capital / be famous for /
Eiffel Tower

1. Comprehension
(a) X → There are 44 countries in Europe.
(b) X → The biggest country
in Europe is France.
(c) O
(d) O

2. Grammar
(a) biggest
(b) for
(c) visited
(d) is

3. Writing
(a) Eiffel tower
(b) Paris
(c) most popular building

4. Vocabulary
(a) Europe
(b) biggest
(c) tall
(d) French

Word Tip

연구 / 요구르트 / 건강한 /
~하려고 노력하다 / (몇) 배 / 보호하다 /
tooth decay / kind / delicious /
choose / enjoy

1. Vocabulary I
(a) yogurt
(b) teeth
(c) decay
(d) times

2. Vocabulary II
ⓐ – ①
ⓑ – ③
ⓒ – ②

3. Writing
(a) eating yogurt with a
spoon
(b) plain
(c) eating yogurt and my
favorite flavor is straw-
berry